Y0-BCT-659

Americans All biographies are inspiring life stories about people of all races, creeds, and nationalities who have uniquely contributed to the American way of life. Highlights from each person's story develop his contributions in his special field — whether they be in the arts, industry, human rights, education, science and medicine, or sports.

Specific abilities, character, and accomplishments are emphasized. Often despite great odds, these famous people have attained success in their fields through the good use of ability, determination, and hard work. These fast-moving stories of real people will show the way to better understanding of the ingredients necessary for personal success.

Allan Pinkerton

FIRST PRIVATE EYE

by LaVere Anderson

illustrated by Frank Vaughn

GARRARD PUBLISHING COMPANY
CHAMPAIGN, ILLINOIS

To My Grandson
Jonathan Wade Parker

Picture credits:

The Bettmann Archive: p. 86
Chicago Historical Society: p. 29
Pinkerton's, Inc.: pp. 45, 68, 71, 91

International Standard Book Number: 8116-4575-4
Library of Congress Catalog Card Number: 77-182270

Contents

1. Barrel-Maker from Scotland

Allan Pinkerton poled his raft onto the shore of the lonely little island. As he stepped onto the beach, a surprised look crossed his face. Something was wrong!

The shore grass was beaten down, and there were the remains of a campfire.

"Now who would camp on this wee island, so far away from everybody?" he thought as he tied the raft to a tree. "No honest man, that's sure. Honest men are too busy working to come way out here to camp."

His sharp blue eyes spotted some footprints in a muddy place. He knelt and studied them.

"It wasn't one man," he told himself. "It was several men—a regular gang!"

Suddenly he remembered the talk he had heard in town about a gang of counterfeiters who were passing fake money.

"This may be their hideout," he decided. "I'll tell Sheriff Dearborn about it as soon as I've cut my lumber."

He picked up his axe and, barefoot as usual, went into the woods to find small straight trees. He was a husky young man with powerful shoulders and arms that could swing a ten-pound hammer for hours without tiring. It took strength to be a cooper—a barrel-maker. Allan owned the only cooperage in this part of Illinois.

On this bright spring morning in 1847,

house sitting halfway up a grassy slope. He had built the long wooden building himself. He and his wife, Joan, and their small son, William, lived in the front rooms. His cooperage was in the back.

Allan's face glowed with pride as he watched smoke rising from the cooperage fires and heard the busy rat-a-tat-tat of hammers. He had started his business a few years earlier with nothing but the work his own two hands could do. Now he had eight helpers, and his shop turned out barrels for all the farmers in the region. They were good barrels. They were so tightly made that not a drop of oil or vinegar could leak out through a crack.

"Aye, it's a fine thing for a man to have his own business," Allan thought proudly. "And it's a fine thing for me that I learned the cooper's craft back in

Scotland. The Scots know how to make a proper barrel."

Soon he reached his dock. He left the raft for his helpers to unload while he hurried to the front of the house.

"I must go see Sheriff Dearborn," he told Joan.

Joan was a pretty girl—the bonniest lass ever to come out of Scotland, Allan always said—but now a worried look crossed her face. "Is there trouble, Allan?" she asked.

Allan smiled. "No trouble, lass. At least not for honest men." He started walking down the dirt road that led toward Dundee a mile away. Dundee was a small town northwest of Chicago. It had been founded by immigrants from Scotland. That was the reason Allan and Joan had settled there.

Allan found the sheriff in his office. Sheriff Dearborn listened carefully to the young cooper's story. "I think the island may be the hideout for those counterfeiters that you've been hunting," Allan finished.

"You might be right, Pinkerton!" the sheriff said. "I'd better go there tonight and keep watch. Will you row me over so there'll be no boat left on shore to warn the gang?"

"I'll watch with you, if you'll let me," Allan said. "One of my coopers can row us over. There's nothing I'd like better than to help catch those fellows if they're the ones who are cheating Dundee people with false money."

Late that night Allan and the sheriff, crouching among the dark trees of the island, waited for sign of the gang's return. Nothing happened. Not a sound broke the stillness except the hooting of an owl. At daylight, one of Allan's coopers came to row them home.

"We'll try again tonight," said Sheriff Dearborn. "It takes a lot of patience to catch crooks."

Allan rubbed his stiff neck. It had been damp and cold under the trees. "Aye. Tonight, sheriff."

They watched every night for a week.

"I'm beginning to feel foolish, sheriff," Allan said one midnight. "It looks as if I've brought you out here for nothing."

"Nay, lad, it's my job and—" Abruptly the sheriff stopped talking. "What's that?" he whispered.

In the quiet night they heard the rasp of oarlocks. Someone was coming!

Then through the trees they saw the

flickering light of a lantern. Soon they heard the scuffing sound of a boat being dragged to land and the crunch of shoes on the pebbled shore.

"Get your gun out and follow me," whispered the sheriff.

Quietly they moved toward the beach, making no more noise than a shadow.

Suddenly the sheriff sprang into the circle of light made by the lantern.

"Put up your hands!" he shouted. His gun was aimed straight at the four startled men who were unloading heavy sacks from the boat. "Pinkerton, see what they've got in those sacks."

"Money! Counterfeit money!" Allan exclaimed when he had opened a bag. "A sack of bogus dimes!" Angrily he opened another bag, thinking how long and hard an honest man had to work to earn a dime. "This bag has some tools in it. Why, sheriff, these are the tools to make the dimes!"

"We've caught our men," the sheriff said. "Signal your coopers."

Allan raised his gun and fired a shot into the night sky. It was the signal for men waiting on the riverbank. Soon boats carrying several big, strong coopers arrived at the island. The surprised and helpless counterfeiters were taken to Dundee and jailed.

"A good night's work, lad," the sheriff told Allan.

To the people of Dundee, Allan was now a hero, and the nameless island had a name. It was "Bogus Island."

2. Allan Turns Detective

Summer came. One hot July morning Allan was smoothing the boards for a barrel when a boy ran into the cooperage with a message. Two Dundee storekeepers, Mr. Hunt and Mr. Bosworth, needed Allan's help. Would he come at once?

"Aye," said Allan. He didn't stop to put on his shoes. Bareheaded, barefooted, and dressed in rough work pants and shirt, he went to town.

The Dundee men were waiting for him in Mr. Hunt's store.

"We're in trouble, and the sheriff is out of town," they told Allan. "We want you to do a little job in the detective line."

Allan shook his head. "My line is the cooperage business. I'm no detective."

"You caught the men with the worthless dimes," Mr. Hunt said. "Now there's a stranger in town, and we think he's passing counterfeit ten-dollar bills."

"Ten-dollar bills!" Allan whistled in surprise. "How would I know if they are counterfeit? I've not seen many ten-dollar bills."

Mr. Hunt took one from his cash box for Allan to study.

"There's no time to lose," the storekeeper said. "The fellow is over at the harness shop getting his saddle mended. Won't you please see what you can do, Pinkerton?"

"Try it, anyway," Mr. Bosworth broke in.

"All right," Allan said, but he sounded doubtful.

Whistling casually, he strolled into the harness shop. With his worn clothes and dusty bare feet, he didn't look like a detective. He looked like an ordinary workingman.

He started a conversation with the well-dressed stranger, John Craig. Allan pretended he was looking for a job. "I'd like to find something that would bring in cash," he said.

John Craig then looked at him sharply. "Perhaps you and I can do some business together."

"How?" asked Allan, like a man eager for money.

"Meet me down by the creek in an hour. We can talk better there," Craig said. Then he added, "You'll have to bring some money with you. Don't worry, though. You'll get it back and more."

After Craig had ridden away on his fine horse, Allan returned to the storekeepers. They gave him a little cash.

Down on the grassy creek bank, Craig questioned Allan carefully. Allan played his part well. Soon Craig was certain that Allan was just a fellow who needed money and didn't care how he got it.

Craig offered to sell Allan some counterfeit money cheaply. "Only $2.50 for a $10 bill," he said. "You can buy something small with each bill, and then get back the change in real money. These people around here will never suspect a thing."

Allan bought some of the false bills, but he knew he had to prove that Craig was a counterfeiter. Craig must be caught by the police while he was giving the bad money to someone.

"I could use a lot of these bills," Allan said. "If I can raise the cash, how many will you sell me?"

"All you want," Craig promised. "I've got plenty in Chicago. You can meet me there."

"Aye, I'll do it," Allan agreed. They made plans to meet at a Chicago hotel.

Three days later, Allan went to Chicago.

He wore boots which were well polished. His shirt and trousers had been carefully ironed by Joan. He looked like any neat young man when he walked into the hotel.

Trailing behind him, and careful not to be noticed, were two lawmen from Chicago's Cook County. Allan had let the Chicago sheriff know about the plot. When John Craig arrived to sell Allan more money, the law officers quickly arrested the counterfeiter.

Sheriff Dearborn returned to Dundee and heard the story. He was delighted. "Aye, lad, you're a born detective," he told Allan. "You've a sharp eye and a cool head. Nobody else around here could have outwitted that crook. I'm glad I didn't have to try."

He asked Allan to help him with some of his cases. Allan was willing, but almost immediately he received an offer from Chicago. The sheriff of Cook County wanted Allan to move to the city and become one of his deputies!

"What do you say, lass? Shall we go?" Allan asked Joan. "Chicago is a big town. It has 16,000 people. Everybody says business is booming, and where there is money there are always thieves trying to steal it. I'd have a chance to do important work."

"I love our home here," she said, "but you are a restless one, Allan. It's not to be expected you would want to stay forever in a wee spot like Dundee. Chicago is a better place for us."

They sold their cooperage. Then they loaded their furniture on a wagon and, with William, drove down the bumpy dirt road 38 miles to Chicago. They found that the city on Lake Michigan was indeed booming.

Everywhere, new buildings were going up. The streets were filled with buggies, carts, and great canvas-covered freight wagons loaded with grain or livestock. All kinds of boats were crowded together along the lakefront. Chicago was a big, noisy, hustling, bustling place!

"Aye, I'm going to like it here," Allan said with satisfaction.

3. Stolen Money

As soon as he had found a house for his family, Allan began his job as a deputy sheriff. It was very dangerous work. The thieves and murderers he hunted down were violent men. They soon learned to hate and fear Allan. They knew he was a lawman who was clever and determined and not afraid to use his fists.

He was not afraid of guns either. One night as he was returning home, a gunman shot at him from the darkness. The bullet went through Allan's arm and set his coat on fire. A doctor treated the wound, and soon Allan was back at work.

After two years, the mayor made Allan Pinkerton a city detective. He was the first man given this position in Chicago. One year later the United States Post Office appointed him a special United States mail agent to solve post office robberies. Now he was working for the federal government!

His first federal case was to find the thieves who had stolen thousands of dollars in bank bills and money orders from mail in the Chicago Post Office. There was not a single clue.

For several days Allan puzzled over the case. He knew he would have to figure it out for himself. There were no other detectives in Chicago whom he could ask for advice. Then he remembered how he had trapped John Craig, the counterfeiter. He had played the part of a man looking for a job.

"I'll play another part," he decided. "I'll play the part of a man who has a job this time!" He arranged to have himself hired as a clerk in the Chicago Post Office. For days he sorted letters.

One by one, Allan quietly investigated the other postal clerks. After hours of

Chicago was a bustling city when Allan became its first official detective.

Chicago Historical Society

work in the mail room, he spent more hours carefully going over the post office records of the clerks. That meant he was really doing two jobs, but hard work never bothered the young detective. At last he made a discovery.

One of the clerks, Theodore Dennison, was a nephew of the Chicago postmaster. Theodore had a brother who had once been arrested for mail robbery in another city.

"Theodore may have learned some tricks from his brother," Allan decided.

Pretending to be a jolly, not very smart fellow, Allan began to spend time with Theodore.

"You're a mighty quick worker," he said to Theodore one day. "I don't see how you can sort mail so fast and never make a mistake."

Theodore enjoyed praise. Soon he was boasting to Allan, "My fingertips are so sensitive that I can just touch a letter and know whether there's a penny or a dollar inside."

From then on Allan watched Theodore, but he was careful not to let the man know it. One evening when he was watching from behind a big stack of packages, he saw Theodore slip several letters into his pocket. That was all the proof Allan thought he needed. Next day he had the clerk arrested.

"You'd better be able to prove your charges against my nephew," the postmaster told Allan angrily. "You say he pocketed some letters. Where are they? Where is all the stolen money? Show me your proof, Pinkerton, or you're through as a law officer!"

Allan and two deputy sheriffs arranged to search Theodore's rented room. There the three lawmen took the bed apart. They examined chairs. They looked for secret drawers in desk and dresser. They ripped the carpet from the floor. They even pulled up some loose floorboards. They found nothing. At last the two tired deputies gave up the hunt.

"You're in a bad spot, Pinkerton," one said with sympathy. "There's no money hidden here. You've placed a charge against Theodore Dennison that you can't prove. Now he can make plenty of trouble for you. You'd better leave Chicago."

Allan looked puzzled. "I know that man is the thief," he insisted. "But where did he hide the money?"

Slowly Allan's eyes studied the room—the floor, the furniture, the . . . "Wait!"

he exclaimed. "The pictures! We've not looked there!"

He lifted a picture from its nail on the wall. Taped to the back of the painting were several large bills. There was more money behind other pictures. By the time they finished, they'd found $3,738 of stolen money. Allan had also learned one lesson he would never forget—always have your proof ready before you accuse a man of a crime.

Now Allan was a hero in Chicago, just as he'd once been in Dundee. A Chicago newspaper said of him:

"For three weeks Mr. Pinkerton scarcely has had any rest in the devotion with which he has followed up the criminal . . . . As a detective, Mr. Pinkerton has no superior, and we doubt if he has any equal in this country."

4. The "Private Eye"

"Pinkerton, why don't you start a detective agency of your own?" asked John F. Tracy. He was the president of a railroad, and Detective Pinkerton had just solved a railroad case in which a ticket agent had stolen $5,000 of postal money orders. Allan had caught the thief.

Tracy looked across his desk at Allan. "I've talked to two other railroad presidents. They've been losing money to thieves too. Between us, we'll pay you well to protect our property."

"Thank you," Allan said. "I'd like to have my own business, but it would mean a lot of traveling, and I don't like to be away from my family."

Tracy nodded. "Yet a man with a family must look ahead to the future. You could build up a good business handling all sorts of cases. There's not a private detective agency in Chicago, and we need one. This is a very rich city. More and more criminals are coming here. They rob and murder, but they're never caught."

He leaned across the desk, talking earnestly.

"We both know why they aren't caught, Pinkerton. After a crook commits a crime here, he just skips to another town and laughs at us. He knows the law doesn't allow city and county police to follow criminals across city and county lines.

Someday the federal government will have to set up a law enforcement agency. Meantime, we need a private police force that can go anywhere and follow a crook no matter how far he runs."

Slowly Allan nodded his head. "Aye," he said. "There's a need."

In 1850, when he was only 31 years old, Allan started a business that would become known as Pinkerton's National Detective Agency. It was the first such agency in Chicago and one of the first in the United States.

He rented an office. He bought a desk, a filing cabinet, and some chairs. He set about hiring a staff of employees.

Out-of-work lawmen in Chicago thought that of course he would hire them. After all, who else was there with experience in solving crimes? But when they learned the kind of men Allan was seeking, they knew they'd never get the jobs. He wanted men who didn't mind long hours. They must not accept special rewards from clients. They must dress in a simple fashion and live quietly.

"You don't want ordinary men; you want *saints*!" the ex-lawmen told him.

"I only want honest men who will not muddle their minds with drink, and who will give every client the same good service without thought of special rewards," Allan said. "I want men who hate crime as much as I do and are willing to work hard to stop it."

The men he hired had never done detective work. They were clerks, seamen, farmers, and merchants. One man was even a watchmaker. Yet Allan always knew how to choose the right people. They

all proved to be smart, courageous, and loyal employees as well as honest men.

One afternoon a slim brown-haired woman came to the Pinkerton office. She said her name was Mrs. Kate Warne. She was a widow, and she wanted to be a detective.

Allan had never heard of a woman detective. Rather amused, he leaned back in his chair and asked her why she thought she could be of use to the agency.

"I can find out secrets in many places where it would be impossible for men detectives to go," Mrs. Warne answered.

It was a new idea to Allan, and he liked new ideas.

"I'll think about it. Come back tomorrow," he told her.

He thought about it late into the night. The more he thought, the more he liked Kate Warne's suggestion. The next day he hired her. She was the nation's first woman detective, and an excellent one. Years later Allan would often say of her, "Mrs. Warne never let me down."

Allan called his detectives "operatives." Before he sent them out on cases, he taught them the things he had learned for himself about detective work.

He told them how to "shadow," or follow, a suspect without being noticed. He showed them how to use disguises and play the part of a farmer, a gambler, or rough workingman. His office closet was soon filled with costumes and wigs. He taught them what he called "roping"—getting in with a gang of criminals and pretending to be one of them in order to learn their secrets. This system later became known as "infiltration" and is widely used in gathering crime information today.

He set up a code of ethics for his agency. Among other things, it stated that the agency would not work for criminals against the law. It would not work for one political party against another. It would not take cases of scandal.

The former lawmen shook their heads. "There are too many cases you won't take," they told him, "and there aren't

enough cases you *will* take to keep you in business. You'll soon go broke."

Stubbornly, Allan stayed with his code of ethics. "The job of the detective in American society is a high and honorable calling," he told his staff.

He did not go broke. He had many railroad cases, and soon he was making news on other crimes. When vandals robbed graves in Chicago's old French Cemetery,

Allan sent eight operatives to guard the cemetery. Soon they caught the vandals.

One day Allan played a hunch. He saw a man on the street whom he thought should be watched. He trailed the man until the stranger disappeared into a hotel for the night. Next morning Allan disguised himself as a workingman. Wearing rough clothes, a dusty cap, and carrying a lunch pail, he was in front of the hotel when the stranger came out. Again Allan shadowed him and caught him in the act of digging up a box of stolen jewels.

Such cases put Allan's name into the newspaper headlines. Soon he had almost more work than he could handle. "I am overwhelmed with business," he wrote to his friend Mr. Hunt, the storekeeper at Dundee.

Allan started the nation's first guard service. It began with six uniformed men who were employed to protect Chicago's meat-packing plants. In time the service would grow to a guard force of 20,000 men spread all over the world.

Since there were no textbooks to go by, Allan had to plan his own methods to fight crime. He started the first "Rogues' Gallery," a huge file of pictures and information about criminals. For years his file was the only one in the nation, and he shared it with all law groups. In time it formed the basis for the criminal identification system of the modern FBI.

Indeed, many of the methods that Allan Pinkerton worked out were later used by all law enforcement groups. But Allan was the first to plan and try them.

For ten years he worked to build up his

The open eye and the slogan "We Never Sleep" earned Pinkerton the nickname "Private Eye."

private detective agency. The symbol he chose for the agency was a picture of a wide-open staring eye. Under it was the slogan "We Never Sleep," and there were nights Allan really didn't sleep when he was working on an important case.

Criminals began to live in terror of him. They called him the "Private Eye" and said he'd follow a man to the end of the earth to arrest him.

5. Guarding Abraham Lincoln

On a cold February morning in 1861, Allan sat at his desk reading a letter from one of his clients.

It said there was talk of an assassination plot in Baltimore, Maryland. Some group was planning to kill Abraham Lincoln, newly elected president of the United States, when he passed through Baltimore on his way to Washington, D.C., to take the oath of office!

Allan's face grew grave at the ugly news.

"It would be no use to tell Mr. Lincoln of the report," he thought. "He would not believe he is in danger. He lets people crowd around him all the time, and he has no protection since there is no government police force to look after him."

Allan understood how Abraham Lincoln would feel because he knew the president-elect. Years earlier Allan had worked on a robbery case for a railroad for which Mr. Lincoln had served as lawyer.

"I'll send some of my very best men to Baltimore, and I'll go there myself," Allan decided. "If there is a plot, we'll find proof that will convince Mr. Lincoln he needs to have a guard."

He hurried home to tell Joan of the trip, and she packed a suitcase for him.

She was used to being left alone with the children when he was away on a case. There were three Pinkerton children now —William and twins Robert and Joan. Allan planned to teach his sons the detective business when they were old enough.

A few days later a pleasant, well-dressed gentleman rented an office in Baltimore. His name, he claimed, was "John H. Hutcheson," and he came from South Carolina.

Soon he became friendly with other businessmen, especially Mr. Luckett who had an office down the hall.

The pleasant gentleman with the southern accent was Allan Pinkerton, playing another part. Mr. Luckett was one of the men whose names had been in the assassination report. Allan believed him to be a leader of the murderous gang.

It wasn't an easy role for Allan to play, because he was horrified by what he saw and heard in Baltimore. Deep trouble had spread through the nation. The North and South were split over the questions of slavery and the right of each new state to decide whether or not it would have slaves.

Abraham Lincoln thought that slavery was wrong. The slaveholding South was afraid that as president he would free the black people. Southern states were threatening to leave the Union. Some were already arming for war. Feeling was especially bitter in Maryland, a border state between North and South.

Allan hated slavery. He called it a curse to the American nation. Now he had to pretend to be a Southerner who approved of slavery and feared Abraham Lincoln.

It was the only way to win Luckett's trust and learn the details of any plot.

Time was short. The president-elect had already left his home in Springfield, Illinois. The train on which he traveled was moving across the North, stopping at many cities for speeches and celebrations. It drew closer to Baltimore every day. Allan knew he would have to work fast.

"Mark my word, Luckett, Abraham Lincoln will be the downfall of the South," Mr. John H. Hutcheson told Luckett one day. "If only something would happen to him before he ruins us all . . ."

Mr. Luckett looked wise. "Many people here agree with you." Then he invited his pleasant new friend to go to a meeting that night.

It was the break Allan needed. That night they went to a dimly lit room

crowded with people who were talking wildly. Here Allan met the ringleader of the plot to murder the president-elect. His name was Cypriano Ferrandini.

"Murder is right if it will save the Southerners!" Ferrandini shouted loudly. "Lincoln must die—and die he shall!"

The plot, Allan learned, was to shoot Abraham Lincoln when he stopped in Baltimore to make a speech. The plan had been carefully worked out to the last detail. Allan did not doubt that it could succeed.

The thought made his blood run cold, but he sat quietly and nodded agreement that Lincoln must die. Then he handed Luckett $25 to "help the cause."

Once away from the plotters, Allan hurried to find out what information his men had uncovered. It backed up his own.

Then he traveled to Pennsylvania where he was to meet Mr. Lincoln's train. He arrived there on February 21.

Late that night the detective was given his first chance to talk to Mr. Lincoln in private. The weary president-elect listened quietly as Allan explained the Baltimore plot.

Then a look of great sadness spread over his tired face. It was hard for Abraham Lincoln to believe that some of his own countrymen wanted to kill him. Yet he did not doubt Allan's word. He knew that his old friend was a wise and honest man. "I place myself in your hands," he told Allan.

For a moment Allan was shaken. The life of the president-elect in his hands!

They called in a few of Mr. Lincoln's most trusted advisers, and a plan was made. Mr. Lincoln would continue his trip earlier than people expected. The program published in the newspapers said that, en route from Harrisburg, Pennsylvania, to Washington, D.C., Mr. Lincoln would stop in Baltimore during the afternoon of February 23. Allan advised that, instead, Mr. Lincoln should travel to Washington secretly late at night on February 22. Nobody except Mrs. Lincoln was to be told.

"Secrecy is all-important," the detective warned. "The fewer people who know about this, the better."

It was arranged to have the Harrisburg telegraph wires cut as soon as Mr. Lincoln left. Then if spies saw him leaving early, they could not wire their fellows in Baltimore. In those days there were no telephones.

The next night Abraham Lincoln and

two of his advisers slipped out of his hotel in Harrisburg and got on a train to Philadelphia. Everybody else thought the president-elect was tired and had gone to bed early. In Philadelphia they met Allan Pinkerton and a few of his men. There, in the dark night, they all moved quietly through the train shed to where the puffing locomotive stood, ready to depart for Baltimore and Washington.

Mr. Lincoln wore a black overcoat, and instead of his usual tall stovepipe hat, he wore a soft felt one. He leaned on Allan's arm, stooping to hide his great height and pretending to be ill. Allan's woman operative, Mrs. Warne, had already bought tickets for seats at the far end of the last car. She had said they were for her "sick brother and party."

As the newcomers took their seats in

the car, none of the other passengers gave them more than a glance. Who would have expected the president-elect of the United States to be on that train! Then bells rang, wheels began to grind, and the train moved forward.

Allan stood on the rear platform of the car where he could watch for signals. He had operatives hiding along the route at every bridge and crossing, for the plotters had talked about destroying bridges and tearing up tracks. If this secret journey had been discovered, there could be some trouble.

Allan's men were to signal by lanterns if all was well ahead.

If they failed to signal, Allan planned to step inside the car and pull the emergency cord that would warn the engineer to stop the train. Through the cold night the detective stood on the platform, peering through the blackness for those important signals. Two flashes—all's well.

They passed through Baltimore at midnight. The depot was empty, the city sleeping. As the morning sun came up, they arrived safely in Washington, D.C.

Afterward Allan would remember how cool and unafraid Abraham Lincoln had been through that long night. Nobody slept, but the president-elect told some jokes. He acted as though he'd forgotten that if the secret leaked out, he might soon be dead.

Allan Pinkerton went back to Baltimore to close up his office. There he met Mr. Luckett.

"We were betrayed," Luckett told him angrily. "Rotten spies betrayed us. We had 20 men armed with guns and knives at the depot, but when the afternoon train came through, Lincoln wasn't on it. Now we're going to catch those spies and give them the fate we meant for Lincoln."

As he walked away, there was a grim smile on John H. Hutcheson's face. Mr. Luckett didn't see that smile, but if he had, he wouldn't have known what the joke was about.

6. Civil War Spies

Now across the country the rattle of muskets and the roll of drums sounded. Civil War had come.

By the summer of 1861, eleven Southern states had broken away from the United States of America and had formed their own nation, the Confederate States of America. Men in the blue uniform of the North and the gray of the South were meeting in fierce battle. Sometimes the victory was not decided by how bravely the soldiers fought. It was often decided by how much military information their leaders had about the other army.

The first big battle of the war was the Battle of Bull Run. There, in the green countryside of Virginia, the Confederate troops won a smashing victory one hot July day. Many people in Washington suspected that Mrs. Rose Greenhow had helped the "rebels" win.

Mrs. Greenhow was a beautiful, clever Southern widow who lived in a fine red-brick house in Washington. It was widely believed that she was a Confederate spy, but nobody could prove it.

General George E. McClellan, who had command of the Northern Army of the Potomac, called Allan Pinkerton to the capital to set up a secret service for the army. Its purpose was to gather information about the Southern army and to capture traitors. Allan decided to find out if the black-haired lady was really a spy.

"I think she is the most dangerous woman in the country," Allan told his Washington operatives. "She grew up in this city. She knows everybody, even the most outstanding statesmen and military leaders. She uses her charm to learn secrets from them, and somehow she gets that information to the Southern army. It is almost certain that her information helped the South win the Battle of Bull Run. She has got to be stopped."

For weeks Allan and his operatives "shadow-tracked" Rose Greenhow. They followed her everywhere, but they learned nothing. She was too quick and smart for them. She entertained the most powerful politicians and army officers. She told them, "I do not love the old flag of the

Stars and Stripes. It is a symbol of murder and shame." Her eight-year-old daughter, little Rose, said, "I'm the darndest rebel you ever saw." Still there was no proof that Mrs. Greenhow was anything but an outspoken lady who had many important friends.

She knew she was being shadowed. She only tossed her proud head and said of the Pinkerton men, "They're unwashed ruffians."

Anybody but Allan Pinkerton might have given up on the case. Allan had no such idea. He was willing to watch and wait patiently until the suspect made a slip.

It was raining hard in Washington on the evening of August 21, 1861. Allan and three of his men crouched under the dripping trees across the street from

Mrs. Greenhow's big house. Through the gloom they saw a young army officer hurry into the house. Then a lamp was lighted in the parlor.

"Come along, lads," Allan said.

The four detectives crossed the street, but the parlor windows were too high for them to see in. Allan slipped off his shoes.

"I'll stand on your shoulders," he told two of the men.

Through an open window he looked into

a finely furnished parlor. He saw the young captain hand Mrs. Greenhow a map of Union forts. Above the patter of the rain, he heard the officer explain details of the map. Allan was so angry he nearly fell from his slippery perch.

Then as quickly as he had come, the officer left the house. Allan jumped to the ground. Without waiting to get his shoes, he ran after the man. He hoped the officer would lead him to other spies.

Instead, the captain headed straight for his barracks. As he went in the door, he shouted for guards to arrest Allan. "This man was following me. He must be a robber."

The guards rushed out before the detective could slip away.

They stared at the wet, muddy, and shoeless Allan.

"He's a footpad all right, trying to sneak up on people in his stocking feet," they said.

When Allan would not tell them his name, they threw him into jail.

It took the detective almost all night to get one of the jailers to send word to Allan's "friends." Allan did not dare let anyone know who he really was, or that the "friends" were Pinkerton operatives. Next morning an order came from army headquarters to free the prisoner. "Now why would they want to let that footpad loose?" a puzzled guard asked.

Allan had Mrs. Greenhow arrested as an enemy agent. When her house was searched, many boxes of secret reports, maps, and letters were found. They told every little detail about the defenses of Washington and about Union army troop

Allan Pinkerton (left) was photographed at a Union army camp with President Lincoln and General McClernand.

movements. They even told how many mules and wagons the army had and what condition they were in.

"She was good at her job," Allan had to admit.

As time went on, the army's secret service, with Allan as its chief, continued to grow. Allan, disguised in uniform as "Major E. J. Allen," spent much time at Union army headquarters in the field. From there the spy master directed all of his secret agents. Allan sent many of his operatives into the South as spies, and he went himself.

Playing the part of "Mr. E. J. Allen" from Georgia, he rode horseback through Kentucky, Tennessee, and Mississippi picking up information for the Union. He was so successful at pretending to be Mr. Allen that at Memphis, General Pillow of the Confederate army invited him to dine. Over after-dinner cigars the general told more military secrets than he realized.

Mr. E. J. Allen had some narrow escapes too. One midnight a young black boy to whom Allan had been kind ran into his hotel room in Tennessee to warn him:

"Mister Allen, you got to get out of here! They going to shoot you for a spy!"

Allan grabbed his clothes and went down the backstairs. He jumped on his horse that the boy had saddled and fled to the safety of Union lines.

Allan sent some of his agents into enemy territory to spy out the location of Southern army units or to learn their strength. His agents were the Pinkerton operatives. They had not been trained as spies, and now there was no time for training. But they had eyes and ears, and

These Pinkerton agents served as spies for the Union during the Civil War.

they were daring men who were willing to take risks for the Union cause. One Pinkerton agent walked boldly into the Confederate secret service headquarters and learned how it operated! Another, blond young Timothy Webster, who was a favorite of Allan's, was captured and hanged.

Allan felt that these operatives were almost like members of his own family.

When one was injured or killed on a case, he was heartbroken. To have brave Timothy Webster hanged as a spy was the deepest sorrow of all. Allan vowed that when the war was over, he would somehow find Tim's body and return it to the North for burial. He kept that vow.

After four years, the war ended. A few days later, while the North was celebrating its victory, a crazed Southern sympathizer shot and killed President Lincoln.

Tears filled Allan's eyes when he heard the sad news.

His thoughts went back to the Baltimore plot. Mr. Lincoln might so easily have been killed then. Instead, he had lived to preserve the Union and free the slaves.

For the rest of his days, Allan believed that guarding Abraham Lincoln had been the most important case of his career.

7. The First Train Robberies

The railroad train rumbled to a noisy stop. Mr. Moore stepped from the train and hurried down the depot platform.

He was a guard for the Adams Express Company. At each stop it was his job to make sure that the company's money-carrying express car was secure.

Mr. Moore hurried because it was cold on the New Haven, Connecticut, platform this January day in 1868. Suddenly he stopped and stared. The big padlock was off the express car door! The door stood partly open!

Quickly the frightened guard scrambled into the car. What he saw made his heart sink. The two heavy safes had been pried open. They had held $700,000 in cash and jewels. Now they were empty. "It's goodbye to my job," he thought.

When he reported the theft to his employers, the company lost no time in wiring Allan Pinkerton in his Chicago office for help. Allan had returned to his agency after the war.

Allan went to Connecticut. There he learned that the Adams Express Company often sent its own money car on this train from New York City to Boston, Massachusetts. This special car was iron covered, with a huge padlock on the door. It was said to be thief-proof. To make the trip doubly safe, a guard was sent along.

"Ummm . . . ," Allan murmured to himself. "We have a mystery here. A thief-proof car with a special guard to check it at every stop, yet it is robbed sometime during the three-hour trip between New York and New Haven!"

He sent for his operatives. While he waited, he questioned Mr. Moore. "When was the last time you checked the express car before the New Haven stop?"

The guard shifted his feet uneasily. "At every station since we left New York. That's my job, sir, an'—"

"I don't believe you," Allan said flatly. He always seemed to know when a person was lying.

"Now, sir—" the guard began. He faltered. When Allan Pinkerton talked to a man, he never took his eyes off the man's face. Now Allan stared hard at

Moore, and the guard backed away from that look.

"It was cruel cold," he whined. "An' I've made that trip over an' over an' nobody ever robbed—" The stare was too much for him. Maybe they thought he'd stolen the money! He gave up. "I didn't check at all," he confessed.

Allan sighed. That meant he and his men would have to search for clues along every inch of the railroad track.

They began to search—mile after mile

on the three-hour route. It was hard work, for they dared not miss the smallest spot. They talked to people in every town and village and on lonely farms. "Attention to detail" was one of the rules Allan had taught his agents. Now that rule paid off.

Near a place called Cos Cob, halfway between New York and New Haven, they found an Adams money bag that had been hidden in some bushes beside the track.

"The thieves were on foot after they left the train," Allan reasoned. "The first thing they'd do would be to find horses for a getaway."

He visited stables that rented buggies and horses in Cos Cob; he talked to farmers who owned horses. At last he found a stableman who remembered that three strangers had tried to rent a horse and buggy on the evening of the robbery.

He talked to townspeople. He found a woman who remembered that strangers had stayed all night at the home of an old man named Tristam. Another woman remembered seeing Tristam on the train to New York City the day after the robbery. "He was carrying a big package," she said. "He acted jumpy."

Again Allan took up the hunt, but now the search was in New York City. He traced Tristam's relatives there.

When faced by the stern-eyed detective, Tristam's frightened niece confessed that some of the money was in her cellar. She said the thieves had known that Moore was a careless guard, so they had chosen his trip for a robbery. They'd hammered the padlock off the express car while the train was still on a back track in the New York yards. Then they had hidden in the car and battered open the iron safes. That took time. They weren't ready to toss out the money bags and jump from the train until they neared Cos Cob.

Allan shook his head in disgust. "If Moore had done his duty and checked the express car along the way, the thieves would have been caught inside," he said.

The gang was arrested and the treasure recovered. It had been America's first big train robbery, and the newspapers praised Allan's success. Yet to the detective it had been just another case solved by slow, careful work.

Another kind of train robbery sent Allan on the trail of the four Reno brothers. They were a cutthroat crew who organized America's first great outlaw band and staged the first western-style "holdup" one autumn night in Indiana.

Masked men boarded a moving train. They crawled along its top until they reached the express car. Carefully they swung down between the two cars. Then they ripped through the express car door, slugged the guard, shoved a big safe out into the darkness, and jumped after it. They got away with $16,000.

Now that they had discovered such an easy form of robbery, the brothers and

their twelve-man gang kept at it. Once they took a haul of $100,000. The railroads called for Allan Pinkerton.

For months Allan and his men chased the gang. No matter where the outlaws fled, Allan was soon there too. He had to be alert because friends of the Renos often tried to kill him. One time a man cocked his revolver at the detective. Before he could shoot, Allan lunged at him, knocked the gun from his hand, hit him on the jaw, and handcuffed him.

Finally Pinkerton agents arrested three of the brothers. Frank Reno and other members of the gang fled to safety in Canada. Allan followed them, but had no power to arrest them there.

Allan was stopped, but only for a time. He managed to get the United States government to ask authorities in Canada to hand over the criminals to him. Allan took the gang to the same jail in Indiana in which the other Renos were being held.

In December 1868, an angry mob broke into the jail, seized the Reno brothers and their gang, and hanged them.

Allan was sorry that the Renos had been killed unlawfully, but he was pleased that the newspapers praised him for their arrest. He never tried to get publicity, but he was proud of having his cases reported after they were closed. He was proud, too, that his sons William and Robert had worked with him on the Reno case. They were young men now, and Allan had trained them well. In time they would become almost as famous as he.

In the years since the war had ended, the agency had grown so large that it now had branch offices in several cities and a large staff of agents. It solved cases all over the nation.

"We Never Sleep," said the Pinkerton motto that Allan had written so long ago. By now every criminal in the country knew it was true.

8. On Jesse James' Trail

As the 1860s ended and the 1870s began, Allan Pinkerton's sons were busy chasing almost every outlaw gang on the western frontier. Allan, now in his fifties, was in failing health and remained in Chicago, but his agents rode "shotgun" on stagecoaches. They fought blizzards and duststorms and traded bullets with murderous outfits. But it was the Missouri outlaw Jesse James whom Allan truly hated.

Jesse was no hero. He was a hard-eyed killer. He "invented" bank robbery. The first of all bank holdups in the nation's history was his work. When he and his gang tired of banks, they held up trains. If there was no train handy, a stagecoach would do. But banks were Jesse's real love, and frightened bankers sought help from the Pinkertons.

For years, then, Allan's agency hunted down the bandits. It was slow work. People who could have given the detectives helpful information were afraid to talk.

"If only we could find their hideout!" Allan exclaimed. Yet he knew it was impossible, for the bandits had a dozen hideouts deep in the Ozark Mountains. Although Allan warned his agents to take no chances, one of his men was murdered.

Then came March 16, 1874. Two more Pinkerton agents were trapped and brutally killed in Missouri by the gang.

Jesse James, the daring bandit, and his gang outwitted the Pinkertons for years.

Fury raged in the Chicago office. Three brave men had fallen!

Allan was not well, but he went to Kansas City, Missouri, to open a secret headquarters and take personal charge of the case. Time passed. Then an agent sent word to Kansas City that Jesse was visiting his mother.

On the bitterly cold night of January 5, 1875, the Pinkerton men went to his mother's log farmhouse. There was a tragic accident. An iron torch used by one agent exploded in the parlor. Pieces of iron flew like bullets. One jagged chunk hit Jesse's mother and blew off her right arm. Another killed Jesse's young half-brother. Jesse was not there.

Now there had been deaths on both sides, and Allan and Jesse hated each other more than ever. Allan returned to Chicago. Jesse followed after the detective to kill him.

For four months the outlaw walked the streets of Chicago, with a loaded gun in his pocket. Allan did not know his enemy was there, but he would have welcomed such a good chance to capture him. Then Jesse returned to Missouri, his heart still full of revenge.

"I had plenty of chances to kill him," Jesse told friends. "But not the kind of chance I wanted. I wanted him to know who did it. It wouldn't do me any good if I couldn't tell him about it before he died. But someday I'll get Allan Pinkerton into my hands!"

Nobody ever learned what fate Jesse planned for Allan, because Jesse was shot in the back by a traitor in his own gang.

As Allan wrote "end" to the case, he sighed. He wished it had ended differently. Of all the criminals he had ever hunted, Jesse James was the one he had most wanted to bring before the courts of justice.

9. "The Pinks"

Allan Pinkerton was growing old. His thick brown hair and beard had turned gray. His health was very poor. Gradually William and Robert took over the management of the agency.

Although he was no longer the "man of iron" people had once called him, Allan's mind was still busy and his days full.

He built a new home—a gleaming white mansion south of Chicago—where he and Joan entertained many famous people. None was more famous than Allan himself, the greatest detective of his time.

He wrote eighteen books about his adventures—a total of three million words. In the books he explained some of his personal philosophy about crime and criminals.

He hated both, but he believed that once a wrongdoer had been jailed, society must do all it could to help the man reform so that he later could return to a better life.

That had been part of Allan's code of ethics for his agency. Now there were criminals who said of him that although he had been ruthless in hunting them down, he had always been honest and fair with them. And after they had served their prison terms, "Allan Pinkerton was the man you could count on to give you a helping hand to get started on a decent life," they said.

Great praise was heaped on Allan in his

"Private Eye" Allan Pinkerton, near the end of his exciting career as detective and army spy

last years. He was honored at public meetings and in the newspapers. Men said that he had met a need in America, and by fighting crime he had helped the country to grow and prosper. They said that his agency—"The Pinks," as it was nicknamed by the public—had done much to make the United States a safer and more law-abiding place for its citizens.

Allan's greatest pride, however, came in knowing that his sons would continue to run "The Pinks." They would carry on in the same spirit of honesty and loyal service with which their father had started it.

Gradually his health grew worse. On July 1, 1884, the barrel-maker who had turned detective died at age 65.

"The Pinks" has lived on. It was managed for many years by Allan's sons, later by a grandson, and still later by a great-grandson. Today it is the oldest detective agency in the nation, and the name of its founder—Allan Pinkerton—has gone down in history as America's first great detective.

Index

92
PIN

Anderson, LaVere

Allan Pinkerton

740712

DATE

92
PIN

Anderson, LaVere

Allan Pinkerton

740712

DATE	BORROWER'S NAME	
OCT 8 '74	Stuart S	5-6
OCT 26 '74	ENZWEILER	
DEC 18	Jace	4-S